At the Recycling Center

Sharing and Reusing

Miriam Phillips

COMPUTER SCIENCE For the REAL World™

Rosen Classroom™

Published in 2018 by The Rosen Publishing Group, Inc.
29 East 21st Street, New York, NY 10010

Book Design: Jennifer Ryder-Talbot
Editor: Caitie McAneney

Photo Credits: Cover franz12/Shutterstock.com; p. 4 Marcio Jose Bastos Silva/Shutterstock.com; p. 6 Oteera/Shutterstock.com; p. 8 goldenporshe/Shutterstock.com; p. 10 Alexandru Rosu/Shutterstock.com; p. 12 aragami12345s/Shutterstock.com; p. 14 wavebreakmedia/Shutterstock.com.

ISBN: 9781538352458
6-pack ISBN: 9781508136927

Manufactured in the United States of America

CPSIA Compliance Information: Batch #WS18RC: For Further Information contact Rosen Publishing, New York, New York at 1-800-237-9932

Table of Contents

What's Recycling?

Have you ever put something in the recycling bin at home or at school? People recycle plastic, glass, and metal every day. These **materials** can be reused to make something new. That means people don't have to waste time making those materials all over again.

Where do recycled materials go? Read on to learn more about what happens when you recycle metal.

Sorting and Squeezing

People must first give away their old metal waste. People put metal waste into recycling bins or bring it to a collection center. Some people find **scrap metal** and sell it to a company that collects it.

The next step is to sort the metals. Some metals can't be recycled. The metals that can be used are squeezed down so they take up less space.

Breaking Down Metal

It's time to break the metal down into smaller pieces. The pieces will be melted down. The smaller the pieces, the easier they will melt. People use a **furnace** to melt the pieces.

When metal is melted down, it loses its shape. Then, it can be made into any shape people need it to be. The best thing about recycling metal is that it can be done over and over.

Sheets and Bars

After the metal is melted, people need to make it pure, or clean. Pure metal will make a better product. The melted metal is then cooled down. It becomes solid in a mold.

People decide the shape and size they would like the metal to be. Aluminum is usually recycled into long, flat sheets. Steel is usually made into bars. These sheets and bars can now be sold to companies.

ST GUARD
RESCUE

Making Something New

Companies that make metal products buy the newly recycled metal. They can then melt the metal down again to make it the shape that they want. The sheet or bar that they buy might be turned into a helicopter blade or a car body.

It costs the companies less money and energy to buy recycled metal than to find new metal. It also saves the **natural resources** metals come from.

Let Others Know!

Recycled metal can be used to make new trucks, airplanes, and more. It can be used to make smaller objects that you use at home, such as forks and spoons.

Now that you know how important recycled metal is, you can tell others about it. Sharing information about recycling may get other people to recycle more often. When you reuse metal by recycling it, everyone wins!

Glossary

furnace: A closed place where heat is produced.

material: Something from which something else can be made.

natural resource: Things in nature that can be used by people.

scrap metal: Metal waste that may be reused.

Index